P9-DGD-137

CUTAWAY FARM MACHINES

JON RICHARDS

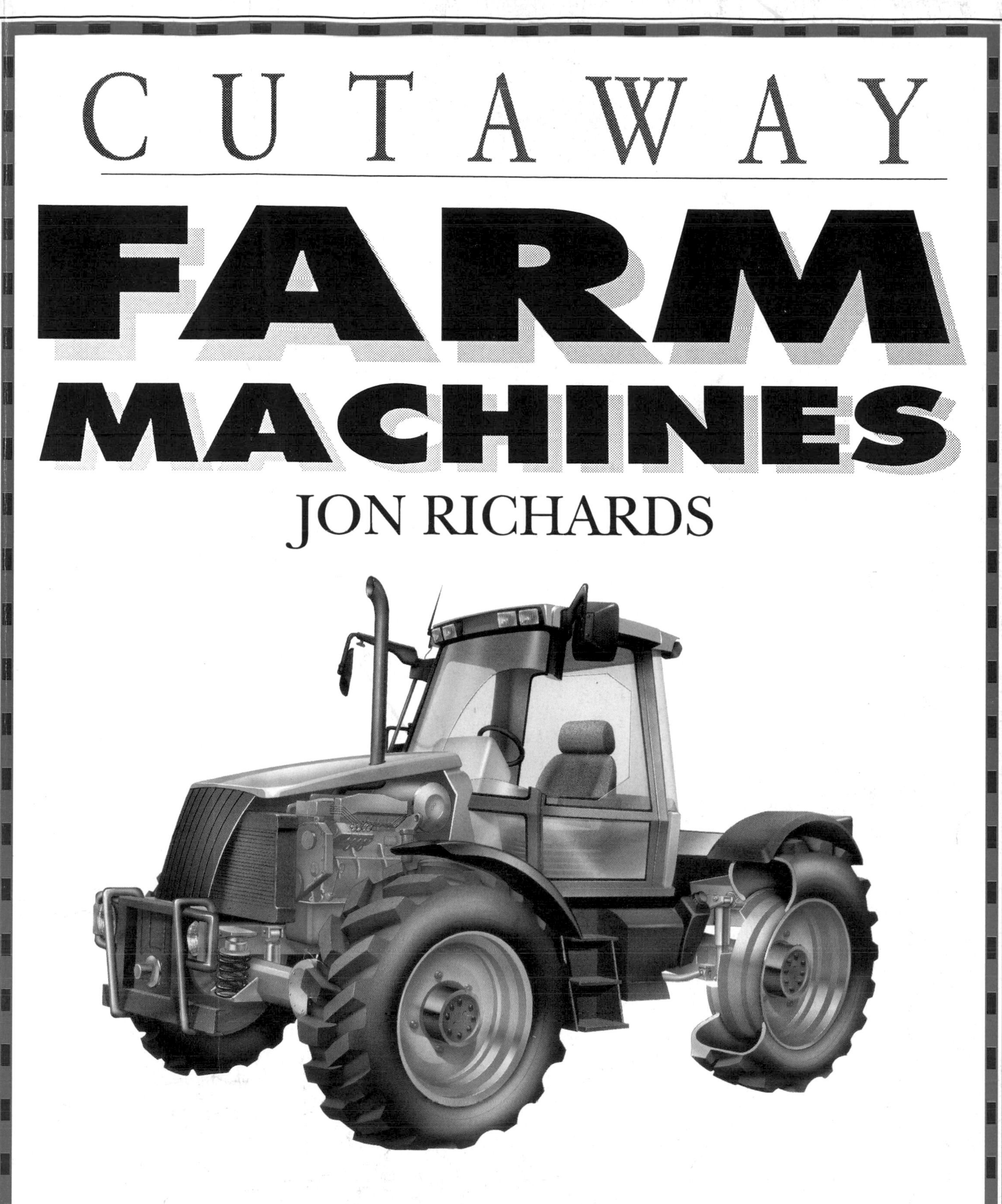

COPPER BEECH BOOKS
BROOKFIELD, CONNECTICUT

LAKE COUNTY PUBLIC LIBRARY

3 3113 01841 1977

© Aladdin Books Ltd 1999

Designed and produced by
Aladdin Books Ltd
28 Percy Street
London W1P 0LD

First published in the United States in 1999 by
Copper Beech Books,
an imprint of
The Millbrook Press
2 Old New Milford Road
Brookfield, Connecticut 06804

Printed in Belgium

Editor
Michael Flaherty

Consultant
Steve Allman

Design
David West
Children's Book Design

Designer
Simon Morse

Illustrators
Simon Tegg & Ross Watton

Picture Research
Carlotta Cooper/Brooks Krikler Research

Cataloging-in-Publication Data is on file at the Library of Congress.

ISBN 0-7613-0906-3 (lib. bdg.)
ISBN 0-7613-0791-5 (trade hc)

5 4 3 2 1

CONTENTS

INTRODUCTION

Farming machines have been around for a very long time, helping farmers to grow crops and raise animals. Over the years, these machines have changed greatly, becoming faster and much more powerful. Today, there is a huge number of different machines down on the farm. These help with many jobs, from plowing to harvesting and making food for animals.

STANDARD TRACTOR

Around the farm, the farmer needs a machine that can perform many different roles, from pulling trailers to clearing out milking sheds. The machine that fits this job is the tractor. It can lift and drag heavy objects around the farmyard, and is also tough enough to drive across rugged countryside in all weather conditions. At the same time, the driver's cab is fitted with a tough roll cage. This protects the driver from being crushed if the tractor should tip over.

Many gears
Tractors have to deal with different surfaces, including dry farmyards and muddy fields. To handle these, tractors have many gears to transmit the power from the engine to the driveshaft and the wheels. Some tractors have eighteen forward gears and six reverse gears!

Front wheels
The front wheels of this tractor are much smaller than its rear wheels. These small front wheels are not driven by the engine.

Chunky wheels
The big rear wheels with their chunky tread help the tractor to drive over uneven ground. They also spread the tractor's weight over a larger area. This stops it from squashing the soil, which could harm a growing crop.

Cushion comfort
Some cabs are fitted with seats that are supported on air-filled cushions. These cushions absorb knocks and jolts, giving the farmer a comfortable ride.

Attachment points
Farm machines, such as plows and seed drills, are attached to special points on the tractor. The hydraulic linkage can be raised and lowered to hold the machine at the correct height. The power takeoff (PTO) transfers power from the tractor to the machine.

Tractors are used for

Towing a trailer

The simplest job a tractor can do is to tow something — even the smallest tractors are used to pull trailers (*left*). These trailers can contain anything, from harvested crops to manure!

Going up

The front of this tractor (*far right*) has been fitted with two powerful hydraulic arms to lift heavy objects. In this case, they are being used to lift and stack round bales of hay (*see* pages 22-23). The other tractor is linked up to a trailer and is waiting to tow the hay bales away.

lots of different jobs.

In the dark

Some jobs on the farm may need to be done at any time — even in the middle of the night! To work in the dark, tractors are fitted with headlights (*right*).

Leaf blowing

Tractors are not only used on farms. This tractor (*below*) is being used on a golf course. It is towing a machine that blows leaves into a pile so that they can be collected later.

Farm machines have

Animal power

Before steam engines were invented, farm machines, such as plows, were pulled by animals, including horses and cows (*left*). Animals are still used on farms in many parts of the world today!

Engine power

Although not as powerful as today's tractors, the first gasoline-powered tractors (*below right*) changed farming a great deal. They were faster and more powerful than animals, and allowed farmers to work a lot more quickly. The first tractors to use gasoline engines were introduced in the 1890s.

changed over time.

All-purpose machine

In the late 1930s, the engineer Harry Ferguson (*left*) invented the hydraulic linkage that joined farm machinery to the tractor. It lets the farmer move and use machinery from the tractor's seat. The basic design for this is still used today (*see* pages 4-5).

Steam threshing

Some of the earliest farm engines were powered by steam. Here (*above*), a steam traction engine is powering a threshing machine to separate the grain from the straw.

Cleaner engines
Today's tractor engines need to work very efficiently to help the farmer save money. Efficient engines also give off lower levels of harmful exhaust gases, helping to keep the environment cleaner.

Front attachments
This tractor also has attachment points on its front. This means that a farmer can power and control more than one machine at the same time.

FOUR-WHEEL-DRIVE TRACTOR

Some of the most powerful farm tractors have four-wheel drive. This means that all four wheels are powered by the engine, instead of just the back two wheels, as in the standard tractor (*see* pages 4-5). Four-wheel drive allows the tractor to find its way over the muddiest terrain. This four-wheel-drive tractor also has a special suspension system that allows it to drive on roads at speeds of up to 50 mph (80 km/h) — nearly twice as fast as other tractors!

Computer control
Inside the driver's cab is a computer that tells the farmer how the tractor is performing. Because the tractor's wheels might slip in the muddy conditions, the tractor also uses a radar system that can work out the tractor's actual speed!

Rear strength
The back of this tractor can lift a load of over three tons — about the weight of a fully grown elephant!

Special suspension
The rear wheels on most tractors are linked by a solid rear axle that has little or no suspension. This means that they cannot absorb bumps in the ground very well. All four wheels on this tractor, however, have independent suspension. This reduces the vibration, allowing it to drive faster on all surfaces.

Some farms need

Tremendous tractors

This tractor (*below*) needs to be powerful to handle a huge farm. The largest tractor engines can generate 525 horsepower — almost as much as a Formula One racing car!

massive tractors.

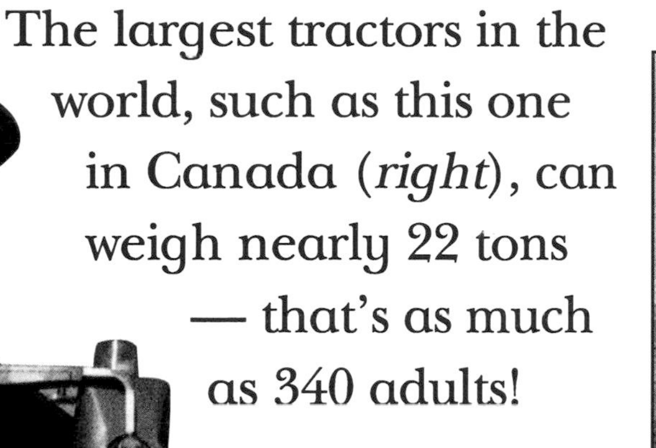

Monster machines

The largest tractors in the world, such as this one in Canada (*right*), can weigh nearly 22 tons — that's as much as 340 adults!

Double wheels

To stop the heaviest tractors from squashing and damaging the soil, many of them are fitted with double wheels (*below*). These spread the tractor's weight over a greater area.

Machines are used to

Plowing

Before the farmer can plant a crop, the ground must be prepared. The metal blades of a plow or cultivator are pulled through the ground by a tractor (*right*). These blades break up the soil, making it easier for the farmer to prepare the earth.

Rolling

To prepare the soil even further, a farmer uses a roller (*below left*). Rollers are made up of a number of wide metal rings that are pulled behind a tractor. As the roller moves over the ground, these rings break up any clumps of earth, push any stones into the ground, and squash the soil down to create a good surface for planting.

prepare the ground.

Cultivator

As well as plowing a field, a farmer can use a cultivator (*left*). Cultivators have a number of prongs or blades that are moved through the soil to break it up even more. By breaking up the soil before the crops are planted, cultivators allow more air and water to seep into the earth. This helps the crops to grow.

Seed drill

The farmer plants the crop using a seed drill (*right*). The seeds are held in a large container. As the seed drill is pulled along, the seeds are fed through pipes and dropped into small channels that are cut in the earth by small prongs in front of the pipes. The seeds and the channels are then covered with soil by more small prongs at the rear of the seed drill.

Satellite navigation
Some of the most modern harvesters are fitted with a link to satellites orbiting the earth. These satellites tell the farmer exactly where the harvester is positioned. From this the farmer can work out how much land he or she has harvested.

Cutting
The large reel at the front feeds the crop onto a moving, serrated blade. After the crop is cut, an auger feeds it onto the crop elevator which carries it into the harvester for threshing.

COMBINE HARVESTER

When it comes to harvesting a crop, farmers today have machines that can do the same job that used to take hundreds of

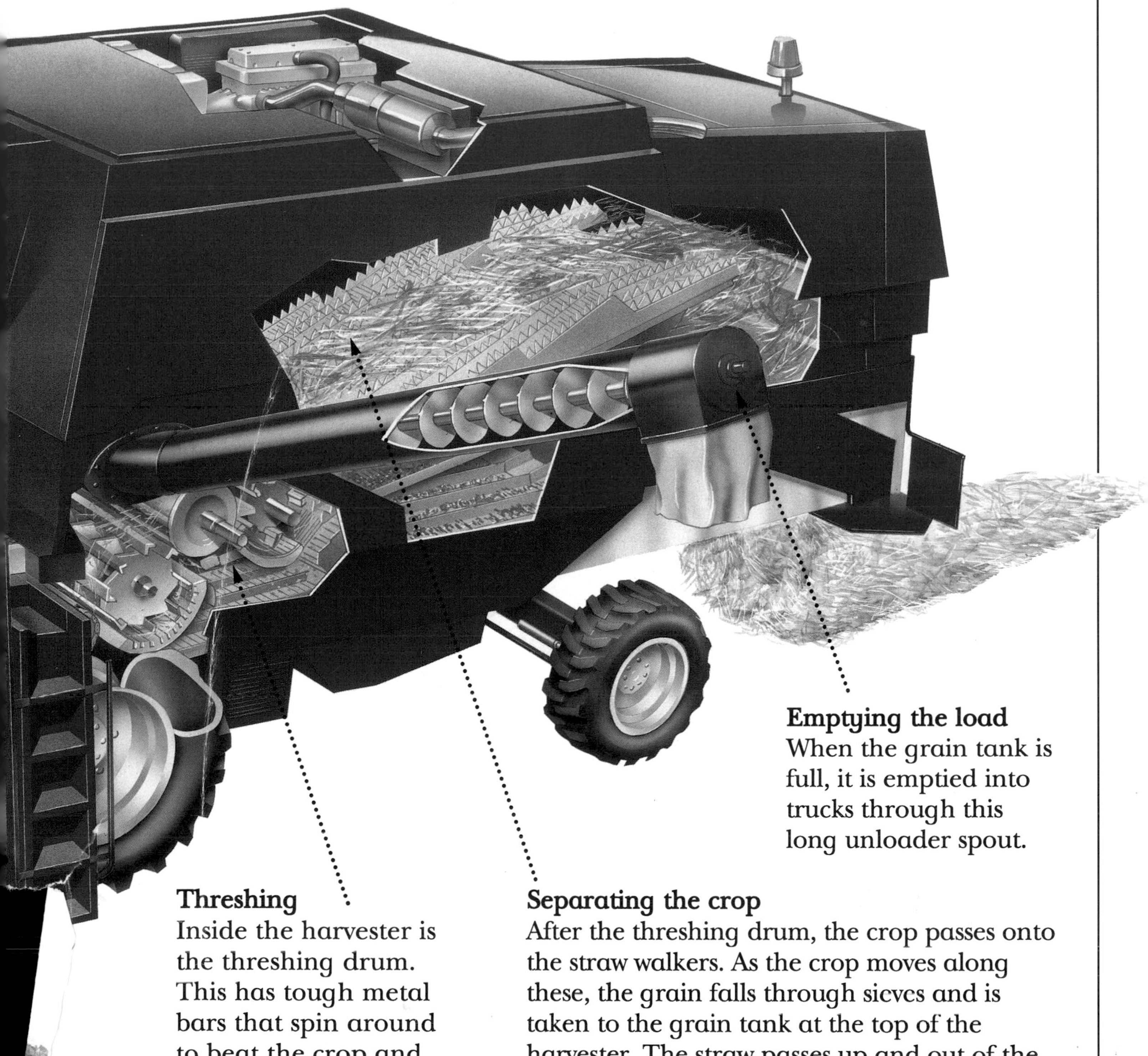

Emptying the load
When the grain tank is full, it is emptied into trucks through this long unloader spout.

Threshing
Inside the harvester is the threshing drum. This has tough metal bars that spin around to beat the crop and separate the grain from the straw and chaff.

Separating the crop
After the threshing drum, the crop passes onto the straw walkers. As the crop moves along these, the grain falls through sieves and is taken to the grain tank at the top of the harvester. The straw passes up and out of the back of the harvester and the lightweight chaff is blown off the grain using a fan.

farm laborers. Combine harvesters can cut the crop and sort the grain out from the straw and waste matter, or chaff.

Some of the largest combine harvesters can cut a strip that is 23 feet (7 m) wide — as much as four adults lying head to toe.

There are many other

Cutting corn

Some combine harvesters can be fitted with different types of cutting tools to cut different crops, such as sunflowers. Here (*right*), one is harvesting a crop of corn.

Buried treasure

Many crops grow underground, including sugar beet and potatoes. They need special harvesters to collect them. This machine (*below*) is harvesting sugar beet. It cuts off the green parts of the plants that grow above ground, and then digs the roots out from the earth.

types of harvester.

Picking grapes

Grapes grow on vines. These are climbing plants that farmers set out in rows. A grape harvester (*right*) is a special machine that drives along between the vines, rubbing the grapes off so that they can be used to make wine.

In a paddy

This small harvester (*left*) is used to harvest rice. It has to drive through the flooded rice fields, called paddies. The harvester has to be small and light to stop it from sinking into the paddies.

Expanding basket
The roof of the basket in which the cotton bolls are collected rises in stages so the picker can hold more cotton.

Engine power
This cotton picker is fitted with a powerful engine. This engine powers the pickers at the front of the machine and helps to squash the cotton bolls after they've been picked.

COTTON PICKER

Cotton plants produce balls of fluffy cotton, called cotton bolls. These are spun out into thread that can be woven

Blowing cotton
Powerful fans at the front blow the picked cotton up through chutes and into the basket.

Automatic steering
This cotton picker is fitted with a special guidance system that steers the machine automatically. This lets the operator concentrate on picking the cotton rather than on keeping the picker on course.

Spinning spikes
The pickers at the front of the machine are made up of spiked drums. As these drums spin, the spikes tear the buds of cotton away from the plant.

Up and down
There are special sensors at the front of the cotton picker that can detect changes in ground height. The pickers can then move up and down automatically so they stay at the correct height. This ensures that they pick as much of the crop as possible.

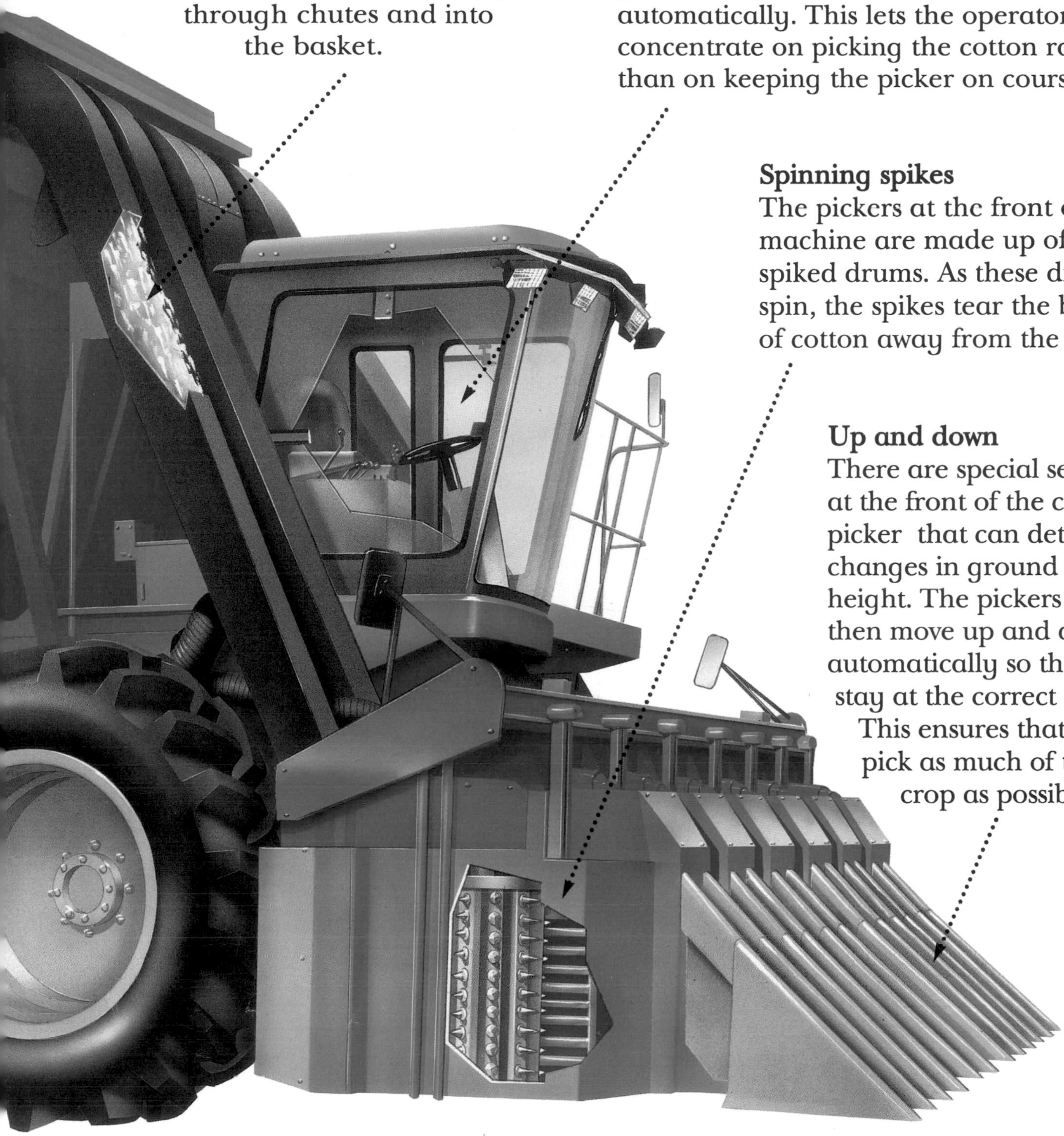

to make clothes, carpets, and blankets. Huge machines called cotton pickers are used to harvest the cotton bolls. These enormous pickers strip the cotton bolls off the plant and collect them in a huge basket at the back.

Tractor power
The hay baler is pulled by a tractor. The tractor also supplies the power that makes the hay baler work.

Collecting straw
At the front of the hay baler is a pronged drum. As this drum rotates, it picks up the hay or straw from the ground and feeds it into the baler.

Back passage
Once the bale is big enough, the machine wraps it in twine. Then the rear of the baler is opened and the bale rolls down a ramp and out of the machine.

HAY BALER

After a crop has been harvested, the farmer is left with a field covered with the stems of the cut plants. This is called either

Rollers
As hay is fed into the bale chamber, steel rollers around the wall of the chamber roll the hay into a large, round bale.

Round bale
Round bales are better at shedding water than square bales. A large, round hay bale can weigh as much as 1,100 lbs (500 kg) — that's as much as seven adults!

hay, which can be used to feed animals, or straw, which is used as bedding for animals. Once the hay or straw has dried properly, the farmer uses a hay baler to collect it into parcels called bales. These bales are either round or square.

Machines are used to

Green crops

Farmers make fodder, which is used to feed animals, from green or unripe crops. These green crops can include grass or unripe corn. Here (*right*), unripe corn is being cut and pulped along with its stalks.

Cutting grass

Here (*left*), a tractor is powering a cutter to chop down grass. As the cutter moves forward, huge blades spin around, cutting the grass. This cut grass is then funneled into rows, called swaths, that make it easier to collect. However, before the grass is collected to make fodder, the farmer leaves the swaths out for a day or two so the grass wilts a little. These swaths are then collected using a forage harvester (*see right*).

make food for animals.

Collecting the grass

As the forage harvester moves forward, the spiked drum at the front picks up the swath and feeds it into the machine (*above*). Here, the grass is chopped up finely before it is fed into a waiting trailer and carried off for storage.

Silage clamp

The green crops have to be stored before they turn into silage. They can be stored in large towers called silos, open yards called silage clamps (*left*), or pits. They can also be collected into bales and wrapped in plastic.

Huge engines
The engines used in tractor pulling competitions need to be big. Some of the biggest produce a massive 7,000 horsepower — that's more than 11 times the power produced by a Formula One racing car!

Driver
Like all other motor sports, the driver must wear a crash helmet and dress from head to toe in flameproof clothing.

Little and large
The huge rear wheels give the tractor as much grip as possible. The front wheels are tiny in comparison. They are only used to steer the tractor. Sometimes, they can be lifted clear off the ground.

TRACTOR PULLING

Tractor pulling developed from competitions between farmers to see who had the strongest tractor. Today, it has

Movable weight
During the pull, the weight moves along the sled, toward the tractor. This has the effect of increasing the weight on the drag plate, making it harder for the tractor to pull the sled along.

Control cab
At the rear of the sled sits a referee. He or she sets the speed at which the weight moves forward, making it harder or easier for the tractor to pull the sled. There is also a switch that can turn off the tractor's power in case of an emergency.

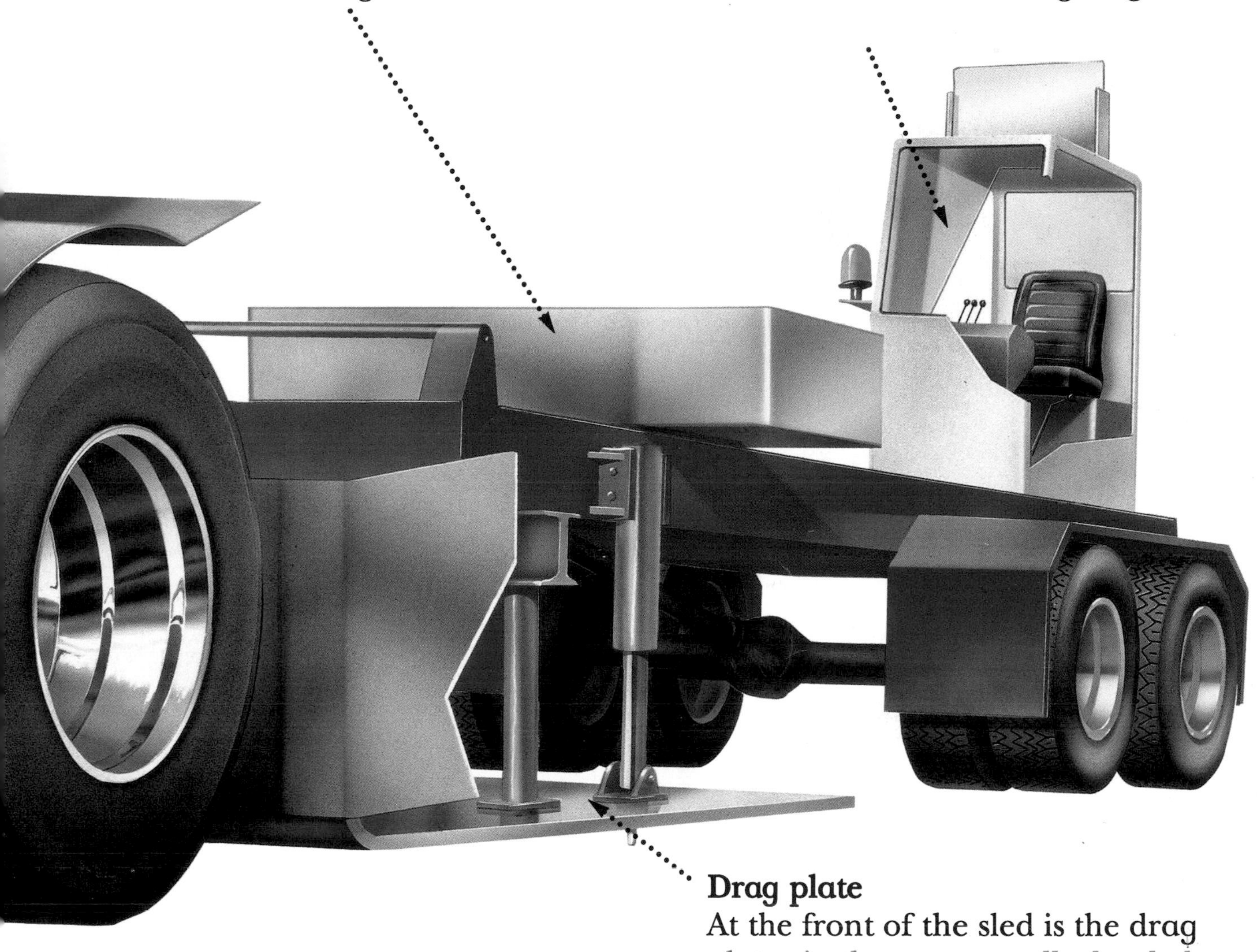

Drag plate
At the front of the sled is the drag plate. As the tractor pulls the sled along, this plate is pushed into the ground until it creates so much friction that the tractor is forced to stop.

become the most powerful motor sport in the world. Tractor drivers compete to see whose tractor can pull a heavy sled the farthest. Their specially built tractors are fitted with massive engines and enormous rear wheels.

Farm machines come

Tractor on stilts

This tractor (*above*) is raised on specially built axles and suspension. This enables it to raise both itself and spraying equipment above the crop so the chemicals can be sprayed properly.

Long arm

Sometimes farmers need to pile objects high. To do this, they can use a telescopic handler, which has a long, extendable arm (*left*).

in all shapes and sizes.

Tracked tractor

This tractor (*below*) is fitted with caterpillar tracks. These tracks reduce the pressure on the ground and therefore reduce the damage the tractor may cause to soil.

Digging drains

The massive claw on the front of this bulldozer (*right*) is sunk into the ground and dragged backward to dig drainage channels. These drainage channels allow water to drain away from a field so the field won't get waterlogged, which damages crops.

Fantastic facts

- There are nearly 17 million tractors in the world today.

- The first successful mechanical seed drill was invented in 1701 by an English farmer called Jethro Tull.

- The invention of the cotton gin by American Eli Whitney in 1793 allowed farmers to grow cotton on a large scale for the first time.

- In 1834 an American farmer called Cyrus Hall McCormick invented the first successful harvesting machine.

- In 1837 an American blacksmith called John Deere invented the first steel plow. Earlier iron plows got caked in mud, but mud slipped off the new steel plow blades, creating a cleaner furrow in which seeds could be planted.

- Two American brothers, John and Hiram Pitts, invented a threshing machine in 1838.

- John Froehlich, a blacksmith from Iowa, built the first successful gasoline-powered farm vehicle in 1892.

Farming words

Bale
A bundle of hay or straw. Rectangular bales can weigh up to 2,200 lbs (1,000 kg)!

Caterpillar tracks
These are wide belts that are fixed to a vehicle instead of wheels. They spread the weight of the vehicle over a large area and stop it from damaging the soil too much.

Fodder
Green crops, such as grass or unripe corn, which have been stored for a time in a silo, pit, or open yard. After it has fermented, fodder is used to feed farm animals.

Four-wheel drive
This is when all four wheels on a vehicle are powered by the engine. Four-wheel-drive vehicles can pull a heavier load over rougher ground than two-wheel-drive vehicles.

Suspension
A system of springs and other devices that makes the ride of a vehicle smoother.

Threshing drum
A barred barrel found inside a combine harvester. As this barrel spins, the bars separate a crop into the grain and the unwanted straw.

Index

PHOTO CREDITS
Abbreviations: t-top, m-middle, b-bottom, r-right, l-left, c-center. Pages 4, 6-7, 18t, 22, & 28t — Massey Ferguson Tractors. 6, 7t, 13b, & 14 — Renault Agriculture. 7b, 19t, & 29b — Charles de Vere. 8 both, 9, 13t — Mike Williams/Media Mechanics. 11, 15t, & 25b — JCB Landpower Ltd. 12-13, 14b, 15m, 18b, 24b, 25t, & 29m — Peter Hill/Media Mechanics. 16 & 28b — Claas UK. 19b — Spectrum Colour Library. 20 — John Deere. 24t — USDA. 26 — Frank Spooner Pictures.